To me, graphic T-Shirts are the most important and most expressive format for a designer or a person. Your taste in graphic tees says a lot about your point of view.

– Virgil Abloh –

Congratulations!

You have bought a White Toner Laser Printer (or at least this book)!

This book is intended to assist you in taking your first steps into the world of White Toner.

The first section is a collection of useful tips and tricks that will hopefully make your "learning curve" a little flatter and get you up and running faster.

The second section of the book entails your active participation. This will be your log for all of your settings and ideas.
Every press and every work environment is unique, and a few changes to the instructions could make a big difference.

The habit of creating notes will also make it easier to spot, and correct mistakes or to look up a successful transfer that you can share with your team or support groups!

I wish you every success with your White Toner Printing System!

- Christopher Sigmann -

Table of Content

There are several different White Toner Printer models, and brands on the market.

This book focusses mainly on a professional level "single pass" White Toner printer like the UNINET IColor 560 or the OKI Pro8432wt

This book does not discuss manually converted machines.

Setup, Storage & Maintenance

White Toner Printers are comparably uncomplicated machines. These work with dry powder (toner), so they do not require regular maintenance or cleaning like liquid inks. This is a great feature, as you can simply turn them off for extended periods of time without any fear of clogging or banding issues.

In case a transfer paper gets stuck inside the printer (mainly when using incorrect paper settings or trays), you can often clean up any potential residue by running a few sheets of regular copy paper through it.

The installation of the printer itself is also effortless. Plug into the power, install the drivers, and you are done. Many dealers either offer installation services or provide installation videos on their channels.

Ensure the printer is connected to a separate power circuit from the heat press as the printer may require a lot of power when heating up or fusing. If another large energy-consuming device (such as your heat-press) is connected to the same power circuit, it may cause static electricity or blow a fuse.

Another source of potential static issues (often manifested as small, irregular bubbles within your colors) is extremely dry air (low humidity levels). This can especially happen in the Northern states of the United States and Canada during the cold season. A humidifier usually helps (40% relative humidity is a good reference point) to reduce the static build-up.

Cartridges and Page Yield

Aside from the OKI Pro9541wt, all White Toner printers have four cartridge slots.

Typically (C) cyan, (M) magenta, (Y) yellow, and (W) white.

Some printers allow for swapping (W) white for true black (K). In short, we speak of CMYW or CMYK.

It would be best to use CMYW for transfers (regardless of t-shirt color) (White on). The printer will continue to print black; it will simply create a "composite black" out of the remaining colors C, M, and Y.

This black is frequently "good enough" for most applications (more to that will be addressed in the color section).

White toner is frequently not required for opacity (blocking the dark t-shirt) but rather to ensure that the printing process runs smoothly. It essentially instructs the paper on where to transfer. Your RIP Software determines where and how much White Toner is needed to print an image.

White Toner Printers will print White OVER your colors (overprint) so that when you flip the page to transfer the image onto your garment, white will appear under the color again.

If you want to print directly onto dark paper or cardstock, you need to print white UNDER color (not possible in all White Toner machines).

CMYK (black cartridge in use) is used for typical office jobs, like printing your shipping labels or invoices. But, **don't forget,** your white toner printer can do more than just textiles!

Now, how long do these cartridges last? Or how many pages can I print? This question comes up quite often, and the page yield is often misunderstood.

The page yield in the specification sheet relates to using an office printer (5% coverage on a letter/A4 page). Basically, a page of text with a lot of unprinted areas. For example, if printed on a letter-size sheet, the text on this page will most likely have a coverage of 5%.

Let's formulate an example:

UNINET® IColor® 600 or OKI Pro 8432[2] have a page yield of:
10,000 pages of Cyan
10,000 pages of Yellow
10,000 pages of Magenta
4,500[2] / 10,000* pages of White – Spot Color

This is based on printing only letters with a small amount of text (5 percent coverage) on an A4 or 8.5 x 11 inch sheet of paper.

A typical T-Shirt design on an A3 or 11 x 17 inch paper size, such as the following example (black knocked out, but not rasterized), will use the toner percentages shown in the table to print the image.

Toner	Black	0.00000 %
	Cyan	6.51160 %
	Magenta	20.60268 %
	Yellow	20.34738 %
	Spot Color	8.98416 %

Since an A3 or an 11 x 17 inches paper size is double the page size of an A4 or an 8.5 x 11 inches, we have to double the percentage values if we want to convert it to an A4 or an 8.5 x 11 inches paper size image.

As a result, we are actually using 41.2 percent Magenta rather than 5 percent. If we only used these types of graphics in our work, we would reduce our page yield by a factor of eight. So, instead of 10.000 pages, the Magenta cartridge yields 1,250 pages.

Out of the White^2 (Spot Color) cartridge, we would get 1,250 pages (when printing only this particular design and paper size on an OKI Pro 8432wt).

$4500 \times 5 \div 18 = 1{,}250$.

Of course, this example should not be taken as a rule of thumb.

If we rasterize the design (drawing these holes or lines on the image) or print different artwork and sizes, we could significantly reduce toner consumption.

The page yield always depends on your artwork and printing size. More color printed = cartridge yield empties faster.

The page yield is compared to ink-based systems still huge, and the cost of toner compared to the transfer paper cost is just a small fraction.

To continue with the previous example, we spent USD 0.62 on toner and approximately USD 4.00 on traditional 2-step transfer paper. And we did not even consider the toner savings of rasterization.
If you set aside USD 0.50 for each printed sheet for toner, you should be able to easily cover the toner costs.

Why, then, do dealers or printer manufacturers provide these arbitrary high page yield figures?

That is an international standard for office laser printers (white toner printers are classified as such by specific regulations).

Enough about the printer. Let's talk about your heat press!

The Most Important Component

Your Heat Press is probably the essential piece of equipment in your setup.

Especially 2-step transfers have higher demands on even heat and pressure than traditional heat transfer vinyl or sublimation.

Quality swing-away heat presses from a well-known brand are thus recommended for the most consistent results.

These are some heat press recommendations:

- GeoKnight DK20S
- INSTA 256
- SEFA Rotex
- Stahl's Hotronix Fusion
- HIX Swingman 20

All of these cost about USD 1,500++, but they are worth it in the long run.

Their heat elements are built to last for decades, so you'll get excellent service with fewer headaches. In addition, because these heat presses last longer, they are actually less expensive over time.

Setting up the Right Pressure

Setting up the heat is manageable. Push a few buttons; it heats up to whatever you want – done.
If the readout is correct (quality pays out), heat is a no-brainer.

But what about pressure?
There are fancy pneumatic / air-operated heat presses that will show you exactly how much pressure you are working with. Look for the instructions (most will show a bar or psi-value) and just set it up. But, let's face it, these heat presses are usually more expensive than the ones recommended on the previous page, and most of you don't have to work with air-operated presses. You don't even have to! The GeoKnight,   the Hix, and the Stahl's Fusion have a pressure indicator and
it will show you a number between 1 to 9; the higher the number, the more pressure you are applying.

This translates numbers into values usually stated in most instruction sheets:

1-3 = light pressure
4-6 = medium pressure
7-9 = heavy pressure

And what if you do not have a pressure indicator on your heat-press display? No worries here; we just need good old parchment/baking paper.
Place a piece of baking paper in every corner of your heat-press, reaching in about one-third to the center.

Ease the pressure and close the heat press. When you have reached a point where you can barely pull out the parchment paper with two fingers, you have light to medium pressure. Increase pressure by about one rotation, and you have "medium pressure," which is suitable for most A to B papers.

Now, if you have a clamshell and not a swing-away heat press model, you might figure out that the pressure in the back is more potent than on the front. This is due to the mechanics of the heat press and a significant reason why swing-away presses are recommended.

That does not mean it will not work, but most clients with marrying issues have a budget-clamshell heat press.

There are numerous transfer papers available from various manufacturers, and even the same manufacturer frequently offers several types of transfer papers.

I don't want to bore you with nitty-gritty details about each and every brand and type of paper. If a certain kind of paper has been on the market for a long time, it means that people are buying it, and there is a reason why it is popular. To provide orientation, I will go over the most popular transfer papers in each category.

2-Step Transfer Papers (A+B)

2-Step transfer papers are most likely the most popular and widely used type of transfer paper for White Toner Printers. Self-weeding papers such as UNINET® IColor® Standard™ or IColor® Select Ultra Bright™ are among the most well-known and widely sold transfer paper products.

These transfer papers can be used on almost any fabric (cotton, polyester, felt, paper, structured wood, mylar balloons, windbreakers) and in any color (dark or light).

These kinds of transfers are the transfer papers' "Swiss Army Knife." To accommodate the temperature resistance of different substrates, you can lower the temperature during application onto the substrate.

The instruction sheets are typically extensive and provide settings for many different fabrics.

The durability is the best amongst all transfer paper types; typically, you can reach between 25 to 50 wash cycles (depending on a few factors).

Within the UNINET IColor range of 2-step transfer papers, you can find different types of papers.
Here is a brief overview:

- IColor® Premium™
- IColor® Premium Stretch™
- IColor® Standard™
- IColor® Standard™ 560
- IColor® Select™
- IColor® Select Ultra Bright™
- IColor® Select Ultra Bright™ 800
- IColor® GLITTER 2-Step™

While some of these papers are great for everyday use and come in many different sizes (like the Standard), others have a more specialized field of service (i.e., Premium Stretch or Glitter) or are re-formulated to work with specific printers (like the IColor 560 or 800).

There is a valid reason for all of these different papers, and the "best paper" depends on several factors (i.e., ease-of-use, empty space in your design, cost, and equipment).

You will almost certainly find a suitable paper for your current job within the IColor range, and your dealer or IColor will be happy to consult with you.

1-Step Transfer Papers

Single Step transfers like UNINET® IColor® Light™ or IColor Speed Trans Light™ are self-weeding transfer papers that do not require a marrying process before applying onto the garment. These allow for faster production and are also less expensive.

The durability is less (about 10-20 washes), and the color reproduction on dark is not as good as with a 2-step transfer paper product. Nevertheless, it is an excellent option for promotional items like drawstrings, shopping bags, or other things that don't need to go through many washes. (i.e., birthday t-shirts or gag T-Shirts).

Hard Surface Transfer Papers

These transfer papers are intended for use on hard or smooth surfaces. Ceramic coffee mugs, enamel mugs, metal items, glass items (mirrors), and other items are common examples.

The application procedure varies slightly depending on the selected individual product. Your paper dealer can assist you with the precise settings.

These hard surface papers are an excellent complement to sublimation applications. For example, sublimation on light-colored mugs and White Toner on dark-colored mugs would be a fantastic combination.

Tattoo Paper and Decal Papers

There are even transfer paper options for objects that cannot stand the heat of a heat press. For example, the UNINET IColor AquaClear™ is an excellent option for decorating candles or model cars.

Tattoo Paper is an excellent choice for either skin or easter egg transfers! And with UNINET IColor you have even 2 choices to fit your personal preferences!

- IColor® Temporary Tattoo 2-Step™
- IColor® Easy Tattoo Paper™

The IColor® Temporary Tattoo 2-Step™ is completely self-weeding means, it doesn't leave an adhesive background on unprinted areas, making it a great choice for intricute designs and fine text. It requires the use of white toner and the B-Part needs to be pressed against the A-Part with a heat press before you can apply the product on your substrate.

The IColor® Easy Tattoo Paper™ does not require a heat press to apply the adhesive, making the process as the name implies: easy. Simply apply the adhesive on the printed A-Paper by hand and cut out the shape of your tattoo with scissors or a little cutter.
It is not self-weeding, so it is best used for designs with a shape you can cut easily.
The Tattoos produced with this media provide a clear foil layer, that protects them during transport and shipping.

The best way to proceed is to investigate your options and explore your creativity!

Pre-Colored 2-Step Papers (A+B)

Special notice goes to pre-colored 2 step transfers like the UNINET® Presto™.

These papers work like the ones used for regular 2 step products, but the color will come from the transfer sheet instead of the printer.

Now, why do you want that? Can't you just print every color you want onto the regular, non-colored transfer papers?

Yes... but No! Your White Toner Printer cannot print the complete visible color range (actually, no digital printer can). As a result, some colors aren't as vibrant as you might like them to be (i.e., reds or black) or can't simply print metallic colors, super-rich bright neon green, or neon orange.

These specialty products offer extra vibrant colors and can be combined/overlaid with regular 2-step transfers.

With a bit of practice, you can create amazing-looking designs by layering pre-colored and non-colored transfer paper!

RIP Software

There is RIP Software available for your White Toner Printer. Most dealers already include it with the purchase of the printer, or the manufacturer adds it to the bundle.

The most sold products are the IColor® ProRIP™ (UNINET) and the TransferRIP (FOREVER), and pretty much all RIP Software will not run natively on macOS. However, if you have a Mac, you can use it via Windows emulating Software like Bootcamp or Parallels.

The most important part is the USB Dongle that comes with it. Please do not break it or lose it since this is essentially your proof that you own a license, and you need it every time you start the software.

But why do they add the software most of the time? Should I buy one when I have a printer but not RIP software?

Let me try to explain what it does in simple terms:

- The RIP Software controls how much white toner goes behind the colors of a printed image. Without it, you either can't run the printer at all or print way too much white.

- It helps you when doing rasterization. Rasterization is a crucial method to create a soft hand, suitable washable, and stretchable transfers.

Controlling the amount of white toner and applying rasterization to the image can help tremendously if you are unhappy with the feel of a transfer, cracking, or durability!

You can actually say that you can't use a White Toner Printer to its full potential without proper RIP Software.

If you want to learn more about which RIP Software to use, there are plenty of tutorials either at the manufacturer's channel or at their distributing dealers. You can find additional tutorials also in several Facebook Groups created by users.

Artwork

There is a proper way to create your artwork with RIP software and any printing system.

Here is what I recommend:

- Create a new sheet in your favorite artwork creation program (Adobe Photoshop, Illustrator, Corel Draw, etc.).
- Make the page size your transfer paper size.
- Set resolution to 300 dpi (for raster artwork).
- The color mode should be CMYK (not RGB).
- The colors are 80% the same, but there are specific RGB colors that might show on your screen that your printer cannot print. With CMYK color mode, your screen is much closer to the actual print output.
- Leave a small space to each edge of the paper to have an easier time peeling it later.
- Remove any potential white backgrounds (i.e., fluid mask), or it will print.

- In general, your artwork should contain some sort of "empty space" to create a soft hand and durable print.
- Big blocky designs are harder to marry, tend to feel very stiff, and crack much faster.
- Try knocking out colors that exist on your garment
- (i.e., do not print black on a black shirt).
- Use vintage / distressed effects when suitable to your artwork.
- Use the rasterization function in your RIP Software.
- You obviously do not have to rasterize or distress every design. But designs with larger, closed blocks of toner (more prominent than three fingers) will profit a lot from it.

Colors

A neat website to find CMYK Color Codes would be: https://teamcolorcodes.com

You can search the website for all kinds of sport team colors.

Another good source would be this color test chart provided by UNINET IColor:

For Reds, I personally use mostly:
CMYK 0/95/90/0 or 0/100/100/0
Creating a white stroke around red helps to make it look a bit more vibrant.

For Blacks, my choice is:

CMYK 100/100/100/100 or 100/100/80-90/0 (IColor i800)

Reducing the temperature during the marrying and application process to 135°C / 270°F can also help to keep colors more vibrant (especially on Cotton/Poly or 100% Polyester garments).

Using more white toner usually produces a negative effect on vibrancy with 2-step transfer papers.

I highly recommend using the IColor Presto™ Paper to print colors like neon green or neon orange (colors that "pop" off the screen).

This chapter contains valuable tips and tricks that will come in handy during the application process on your heat-press.

Training Wheel Technique:
For a successful A to B transfer, it is recommended to peel in a certain way. Some videos show you how to peel for each paper, but many people, especially beginners, don't know what the "correct" peeling technique is.

Here are the critical points for a successful peel during the marrying process, so you can better understand what these videos are attempting to convey:

- Never let the paper leave the lower platen
- Peel at a flat angle, do not go up at the end
- Do not stop during the peeling process. Rasterized artwork tends to clog up in the areas where you stop.
- Peel at a steady pace; do not increase your speed abruptly if you have areas with no or little toner. To avoid the ripping of smaller details, try to peel at the same speed from start to finish.

The last point usually requires some practice and "feel" before you can do it correctly. The "Training Wheel" is a helpful tool for training yourself to maintain a consistent peeling speed.

The "Training Wheel" is essentially an 8 to 10 mm thick stripe that runs along the long edge of your transfer from top to bottom. You can place this "training wheel" line on both long sides of your transfer if your design allows it. These training wheels will provide consistent resistance throughout the sheet, preventing you from involuntarily speeding up at parts with lower resistance – allowing you to keep small details and edges on the A-Foil rather than the B- Paper.

Before the lines are transferred to the garment, they will be cut off.

I've included an example on the side for your convenience.:

DESIGN

← TRAINING WHEELS

White Only Transfers:
Transfers with a higher concentration of white toner, or even white-only designs, can be difficult to peel from the garment.

The key to success here is in the marrying process (A to B) rather than in the actual application of the garment.

White Toner requires a bit more pressure when marrying A to B to attract enough of the adhesive from the B-Sheet.

Please inspect the B-Sheet to see if the release was clean or if some speckles were left on the B-Sheet to identify a successful paper marriage. If there are speckles on the B-Sheet, the marriage was unsuccessful, and your transfer may be difficult to peel from the garment. If this occurs, please increase the pressure on the marrying process.

Dye Migration:

Dye migration is something that can happen quickly if you don't pay attention to the fabric content you are pressing on. Dye migration dulls your colors and makes the transfer appear "dirty" or less opaque. If this occurs, your garment most likely contained polyester fibers.

Colored polyester is dyed with sublimation dyes, which can be released with enough heat (over 270° F) so they re-sublimate into your transfer.

A simple trick that helps is to check the labels before you press your transfers on the garment. If it contains parts that aren't cotton, please reduce the temperature to 270° F or lower (check instructions for exact values), and your colors will stay nice and vibrant.

White Toner Transfer Support Group Webinar:

Many of these tips have also been shown during a live Webinar for the "White Toner Transfer Support Group" on Facebook.

I hope these recordings of the Webinar will help you understand the techniques in this book easier and help you improving your skills. Please scan the code below for a direct link to the group's YouTube channel:

Removing Mistakes:
Yes, mistakes happen, and there is a way to remove the transfer from your garment.

Heat-resistant tape (similar to that used to transfer images onto mugs) can be pressed on top of the error (like a spelling mistake, a white, adhesive line because we did not trim the edges completely, etc.). However, if you remove the tape while it is still hot, the adhesive will not have enough hold to stay on the garment and will stick to our tape.

If you need to remove more extensive areas, you can use an unused A-Foil in the same manner. Again, some light residue may remain visible, but it will be much less noticeable and can be pressed over with a proper transfer.

The White Toner Masterclass
Richard Shannon's "White Toner Masterclass" is something I would recommend to every beginner who is just getting started with the printer or the decorating industry in general. Information about the class can be located via the UNINET IColor website at: www.icolorprint.com
Richard provides hours of valuable tips and tricks, training on the ProRIP Software, and explains everything in an easy-to-understand manner.

Sometimes our beautiful t-shirts need to be washed. But how, what is recommended, and what can I do to preserve the colors to look good for much longer?

Instructions provide pointers

Check the instructions of the transfer paper to be sure. Most papers do come with a wash and care recommendation.

Temperature

The recommended temperature is 40°C / 105°F to be warm washed. Try to avoid steaming hot water as it wears down the garment and the transferred image quicker. Also, bleaching components present in most powder detergents are getting activated past 60°C / 140°F.

Bleach

Do not add any additional bleach! It will discolor the toner.

Reduce Water Pressure

High water pressure in your washing machine will press against closed areas of your transfer, and it will likely create cracks. One way to reduce the water pressure in the machine is to design with empty space in mind (i.e., rasterization).

The other way is to set the max—spinning cycle speed to 800 rpm on the machine.

Washing inside out also helps to reduce the abrasion during the wash.

Drying

The best way would be to hang dry. Drying in the machine puts excess stress on the garments, and they often shrink quite a bit during the first few drying cycles. Unfortunately, the transfer onto the garment will not shrink to the same extent, leading to early cracking.

If you can't avoid drying it in a drying machine, the line rasterization will allow the printed image to shrink together with the fabric; this way, it will not be forced to crack.

When possible, use shorter drying cycles and use gentle, delicate settings. Excess drying will dry out the thermo-reactive adhesive/polymer film bonding the image to your garment. This will shorten the overall life expectancy of your transfers.

I've met a wide range of t-shirt printers at shows and workshops throughout my career, and they frequently ask me about my personal setting preferences and why I use specific TransferRIP settings.

Meanwhile, I usually use the same settings on each graphic, with a few minor tweaks here and there.

For those of you who use TransferRIP:

Step 3

- I knock out the garment color
- I increase saturation by +5 to +20% if I rasterize my artwork. This is because I want it to look slightly oversaturated to balance out the color vibrancy loss that happens during the rasterization process. How much exactly? It always depends on the artwork.

Step 4

This is easy. 150-1-1-partial transparency box is always checked—no matter what t-shirt color, white is always on.

Step 5

This is trickier. I don't rasterize fine artwork like text or artwork that already contains enough open space.

For dark garments, my raster choice depends on the artwork. For example, suppose it is a vector-type artwork with somewhat blocky colors. In that case, I don't want to destroy the proportions of the colors, so I would choose a micro mask (a typical example would be a national flag with flat, blocky colors) with vertical lines, 30 lpi, and 20 to 22% micro-mask.

Photographic artwork with many gradients is usually rasterized using the variable "mask for dark media." Also, similar to the above, instead of a micro mask percentage, I use a shadow tolerance of 100 to 175 (use the preview).

I use the micro mask more frequently on light garments (same as above).

The mask for bright transfer paper gets only used with monochrome portraits/pencil drawings onto white shirts.

Now that you've had your fill of my favorite settings, it's time to find yours! The pages that follow are intended to serve as a log for you to track your progress!

I wish you every success with your white toner transfer printer!

Substrate: 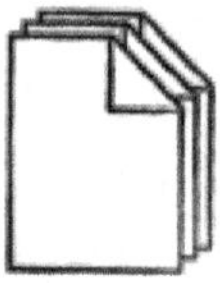 _____   Paper: _____

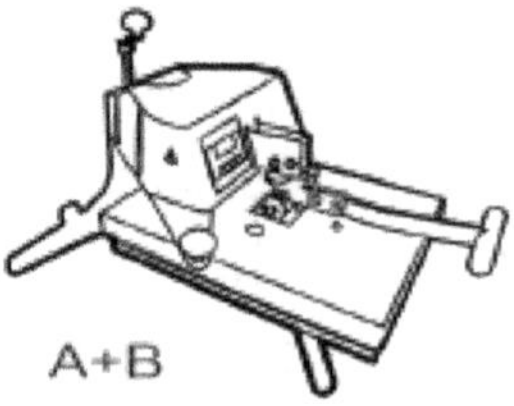

A+B

Temp: _____

Pressure: _____

Time: _____

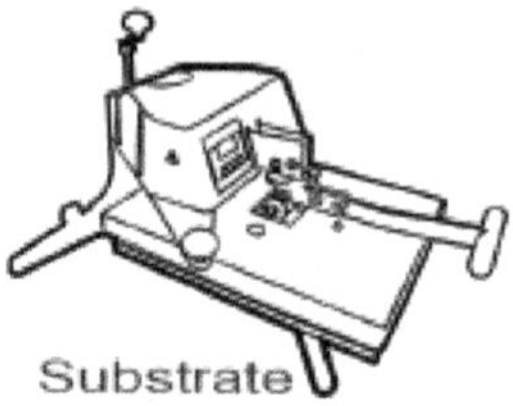

Substrate

Temp: _____

Pressure: _____

Time: _____

Peel: _____

Notes: _____

_____

_____

_____

_____

_____

_____

_____

_____

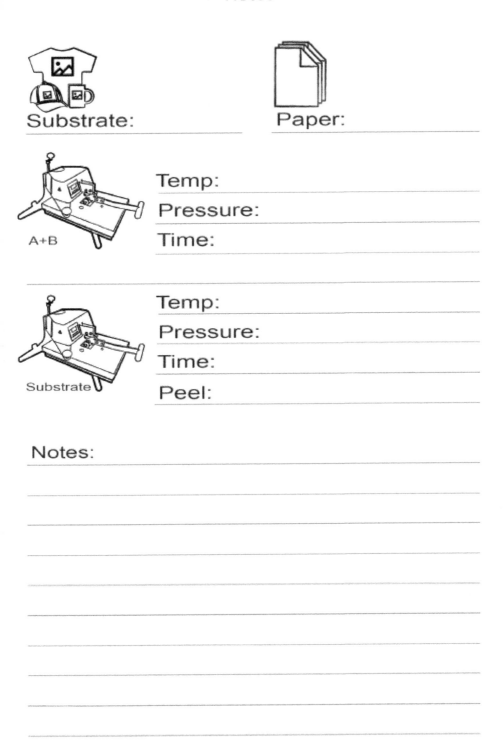

Substrate:

Paper:

A+B

Temp:

Pressure:

Time:

Substrate

Temp:

Pressure:

Time:

Peel:

Notes:

Substrate: 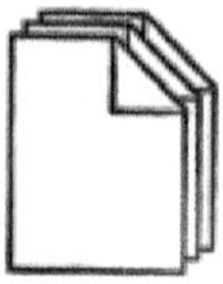 _____   Paper: _____

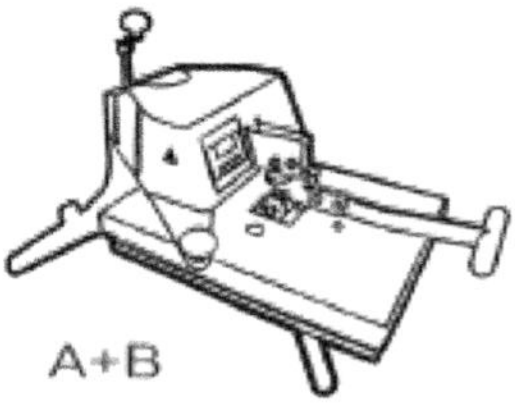

A+B

Temp: _____

Pressure: _____

Time: _____

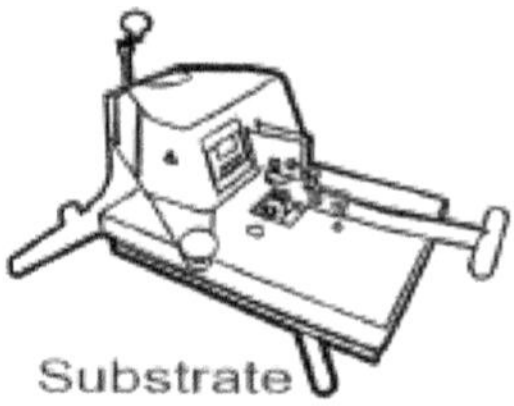

Substrate

Temp: _____

Pressure: _____

Time: _____

Peel: _____

Notes: _____

_____

_____

_____

_____

_____

_____

_____

_____

_____

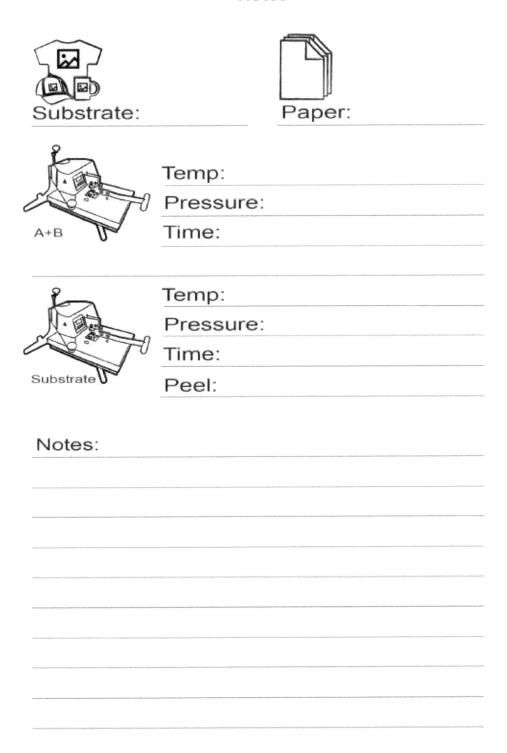

Substrate: _____

Paper: _____

A+B

Temp: _____
Pressure: _____
Time: _____

Substrate

Temp: _____
Pressure: _____
Time: _____
Peel: _____

Notes:
_____
_____
_____
_____
_____
_____
_____
_____
_____
_____

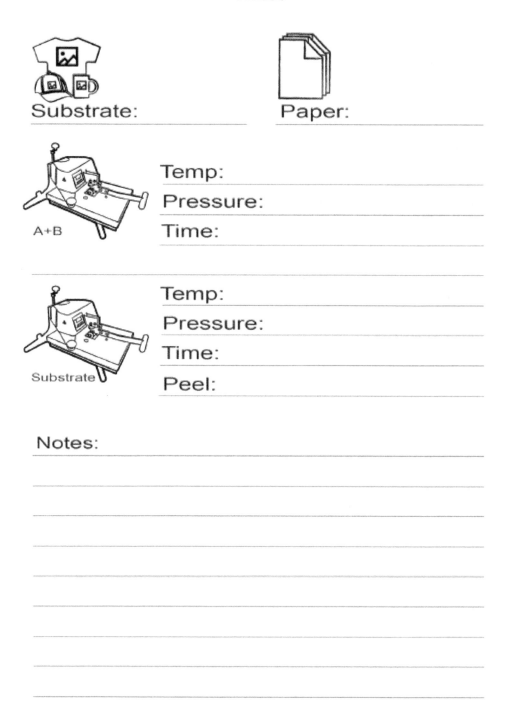

Substrate: _____

Paper: _____

A+B

Temp: _____

Pressure: _____

Time: _____

Substrate

Temp: _____

Pressure: _____

Time: _____

Peel: _____

Notes:

_____

_____

_____

_____

_____

_____

_____

_____

_____

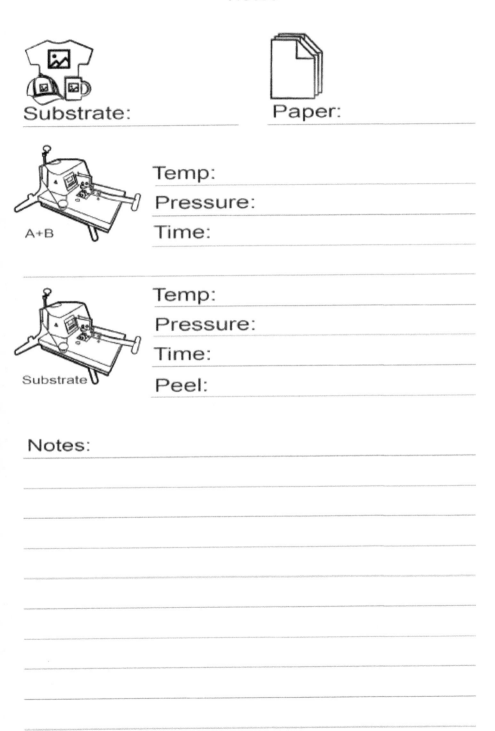

Substrate: _____

Paper: _____

A+B

Temp: _____
Pressure: _____
Time: _____

Substrate

Temp: _____
Pressure: _____
Time: _____
Peel: _____

Notes: _____

Substrate:

Paper:

Temp:

Pressure:

A+B   Time:

Temp:

Pressure:

Time:

Substrate   Peel:

Notes:

Substrate: _____

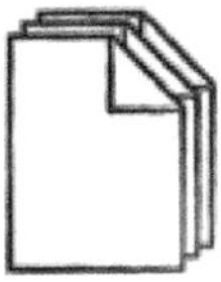

Paper: _____

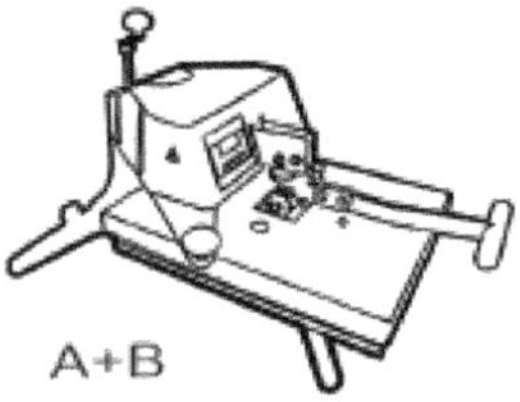

A+B

Temp: _____

Pressure: _____

Time: _____

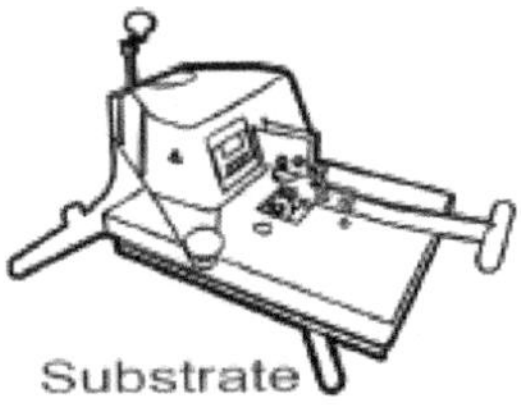

Substrate

Temp: _____

Pressure: _____

Time: _____

Peel: _____

Notes: _____

_____

_____

_____

_____

_____

_____

_____

_____

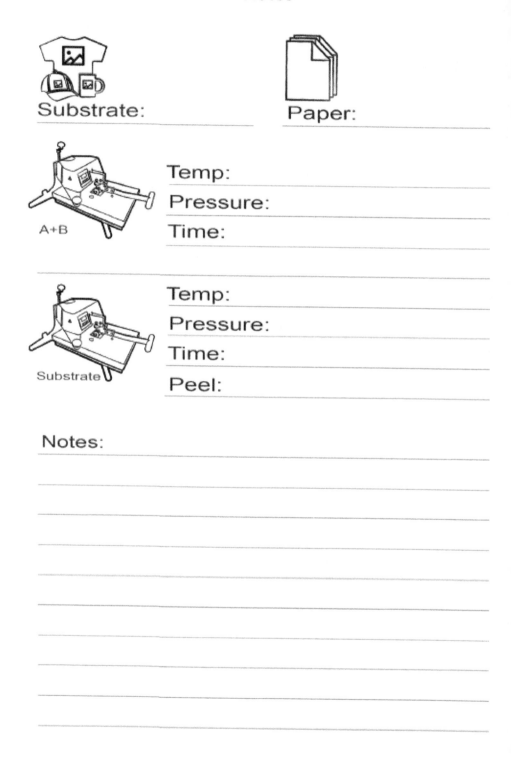

Substrate:

Paper:

A+B

Temp:

Pressure:

Time:

Substrate

Temp:

Pressure:

Time:

Peel:

Notes:

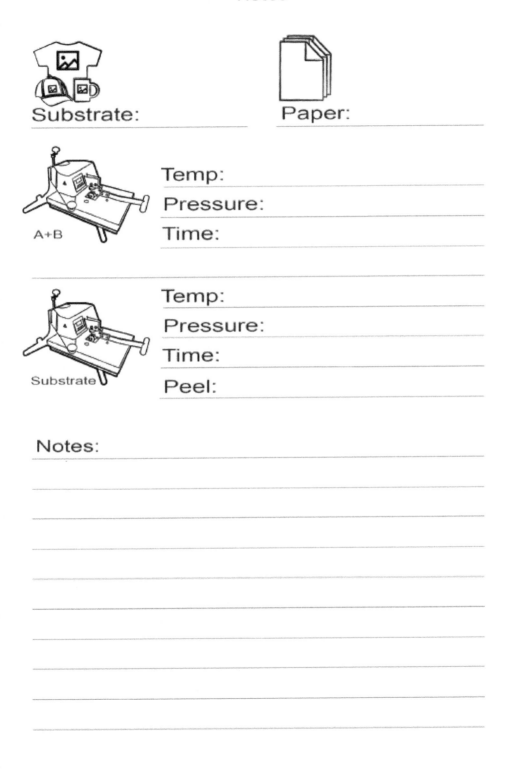

Substrate: _____

Paper: _____

A+B

Temp: _____

Pressure: _____

Time: _____

Substrate

Temp: _____

Pressure: _____

Time: _____

Peel: _____

Notes:

_____

_____

_____

_____

_____

_____

_____

_____

_____

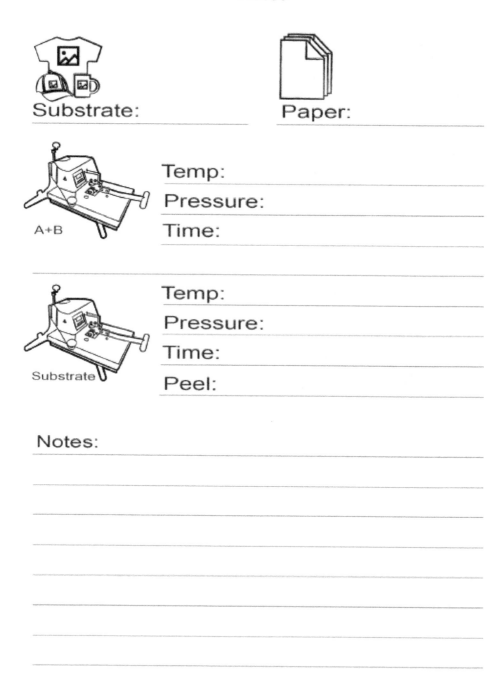

Substrate: _____ Paper: _____

A+B
Temp: _____
Pressure: _____
Time: _____

Substrate
Temp: _____
Pressure: _____
Time: _____
Peel: _____

Notes:
_____
_____
_____
_____
_____
_____
_____
_____
_____
_____

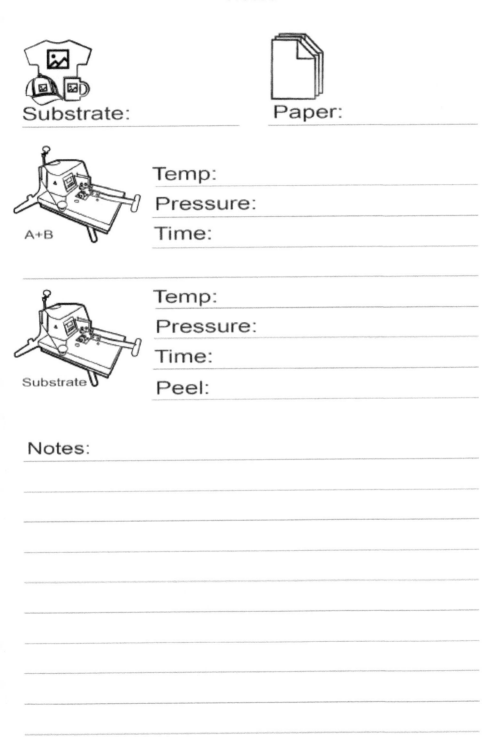

Substrate:

Paper:

A+B

Temp:

Pressure:

Time:

Substrate

Temp:

Pressure:

Time:

Peel:

Notes:

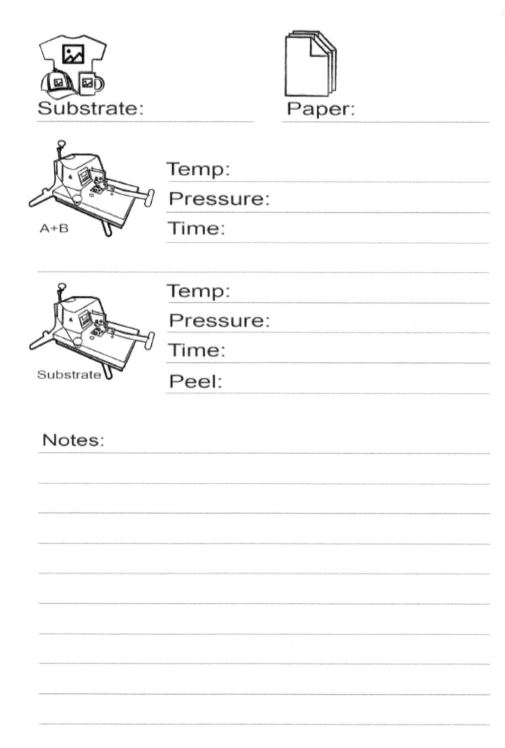

Substrate:

Paper:

A+B

Temp:

Pressure:

Time:

Substrate

Temp:

Pressure:

Time:

Peel:

Notes:

Substrate: _____

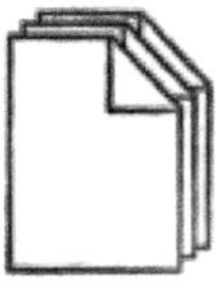

Paper: _____

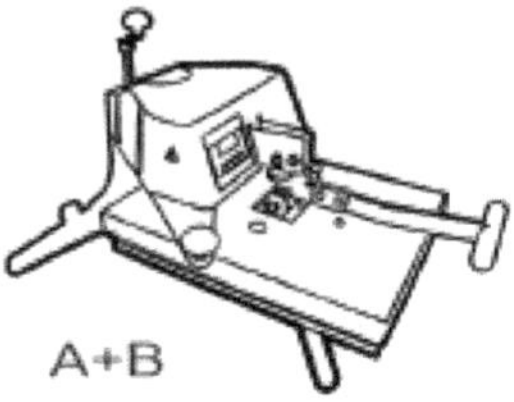

A+B

Temp: _____

Pressure: _____

Time: _____

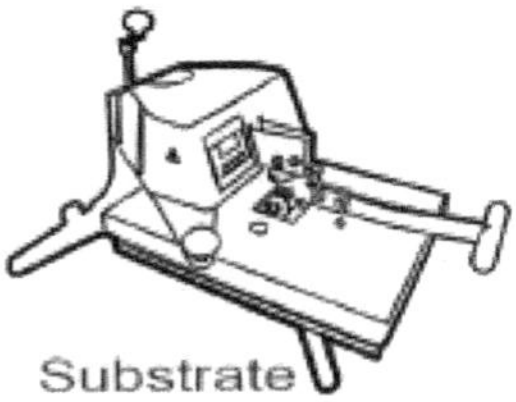

Substrate

Temp: _____

Pressure: _____

Time: _____

Peel: _____

Notes: _____

_____

_____

_____

_____

_____

_____

_____

_____

_____

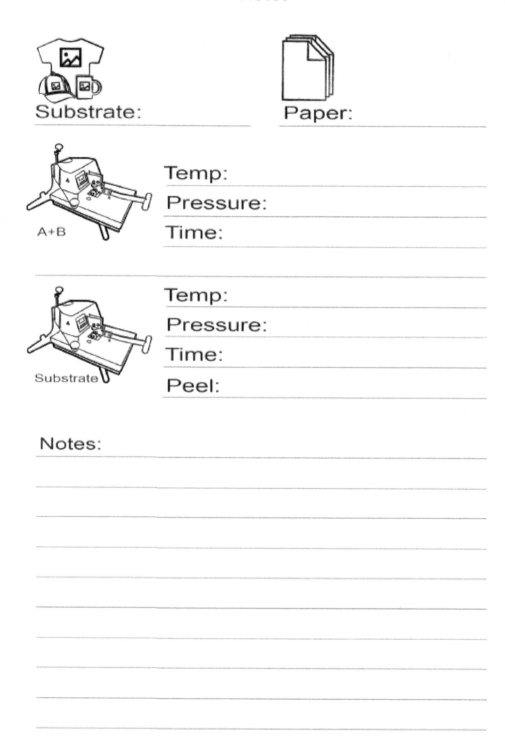

Substrate: _____

Paper: _____

A+B

Temp: _____
Pressure: _____
Time: _____

Substrate

Temp: _____
Pressure: _____
Time: _____
Peel: _____

Notes:

Notes

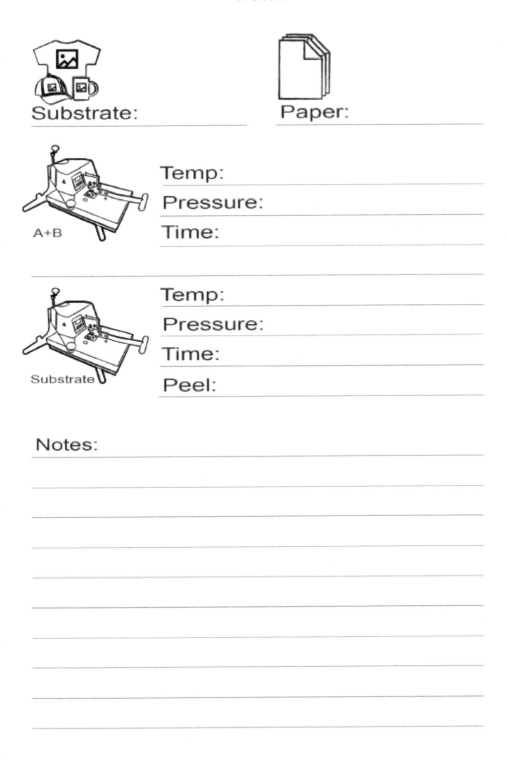

Substrate:

Paper:

Temp:

Pressure:

Time:

A+B

Temp:

Pressure:

Time:

Peel:

Substrate

Notes:

45

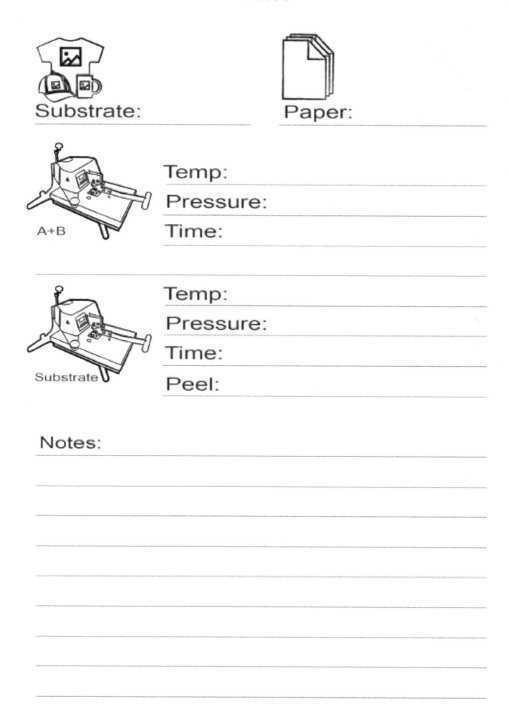

Substrate:

Paper:

A+B

Temp:

Pressure:

Time:

Substrate

Temp:

Pressure:

Time:

Peel:

Notes:

Substrate:

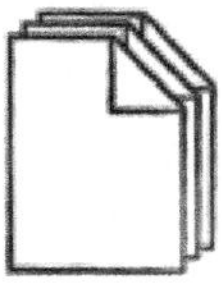

Paper:

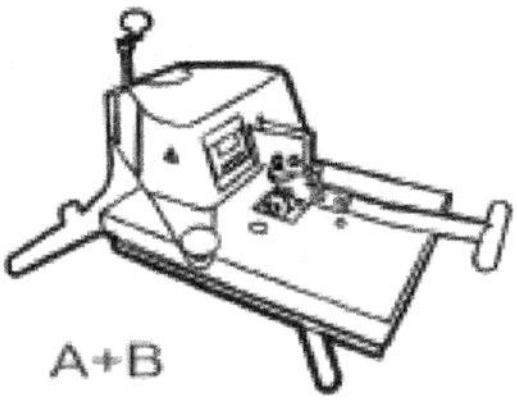

A+B

Temp:

Pressure:

Time:

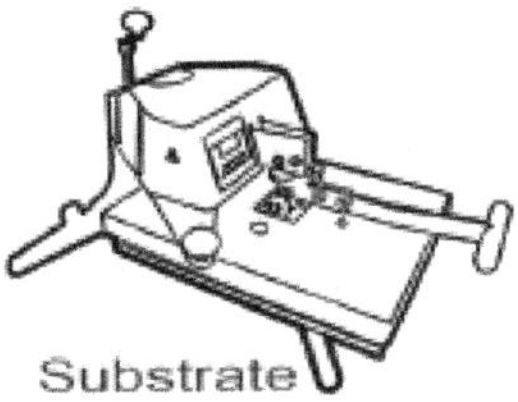

Substrate

Temp:

Pressure:

Time:

Peel:

Notes:

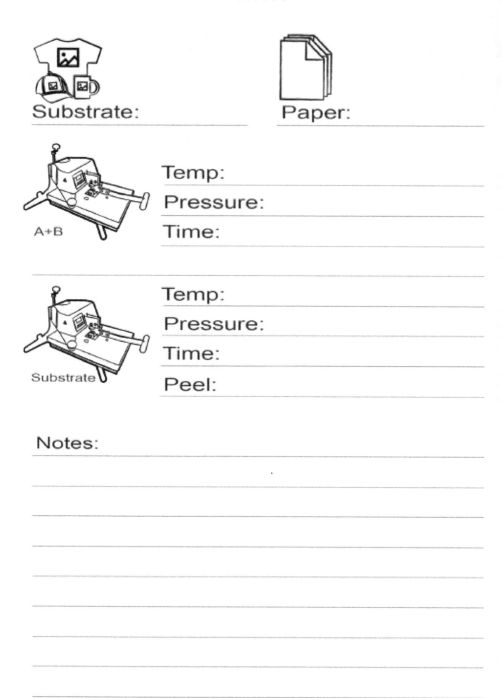

Substrate:

Paper:

Temp:

Pressure:

Time:

A+B

Temp:

Pressure:

Time:

Peel:

Substrate

Notes:

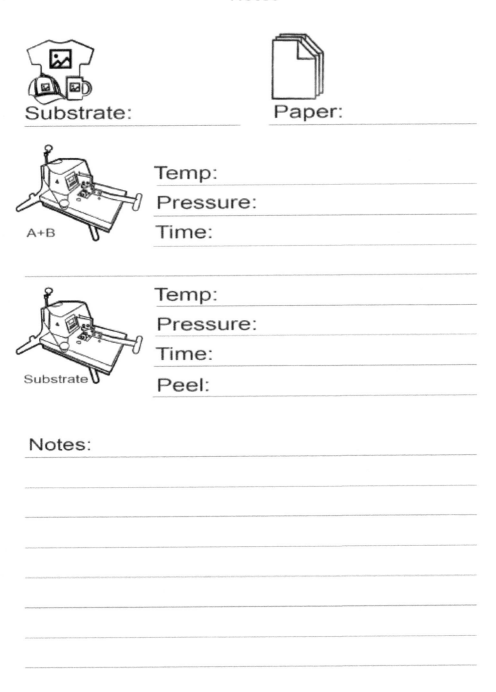

Substrate:

Paper:

A+B

Temp:

Pressure:

Time:

Substrate

Temp:

Pressure:

Time:

Peel:

Notes:

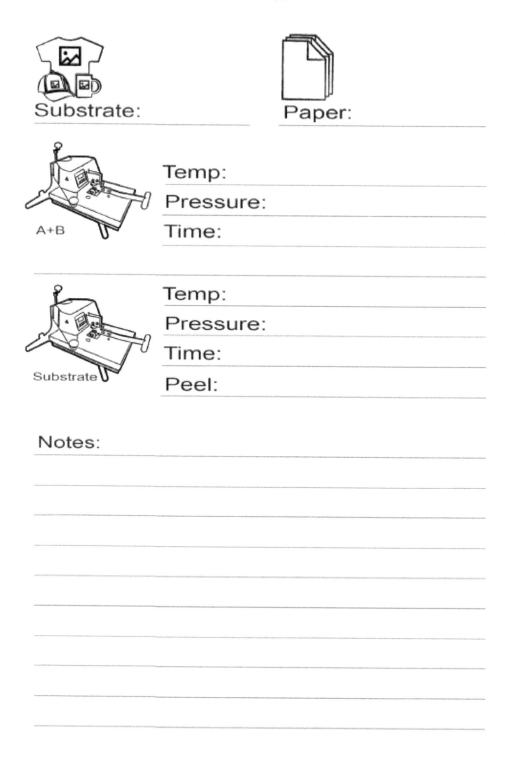

Substrate:

Paper:

A+B

Temp:

Pressure:

Time:

Substrate

Temp:

Pressure:

Time:

Peel:

Notes:

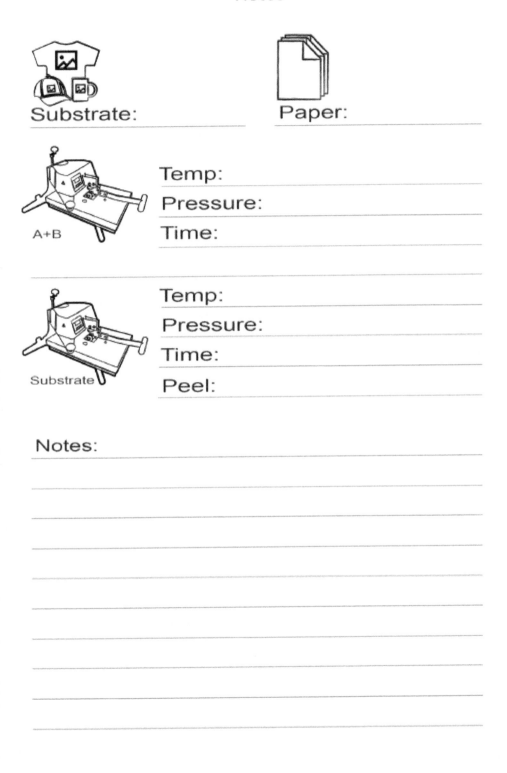

Substrate: _____

Paper: _____

A+B

Temp: _____

Pressure: _____

Time: _____

Substrate

Temp: _____

Pressure: _____

Time: _____

Peel: _____

Notes: _____

_____

_____

_____

_____

_____

_____

_____

_____

_____

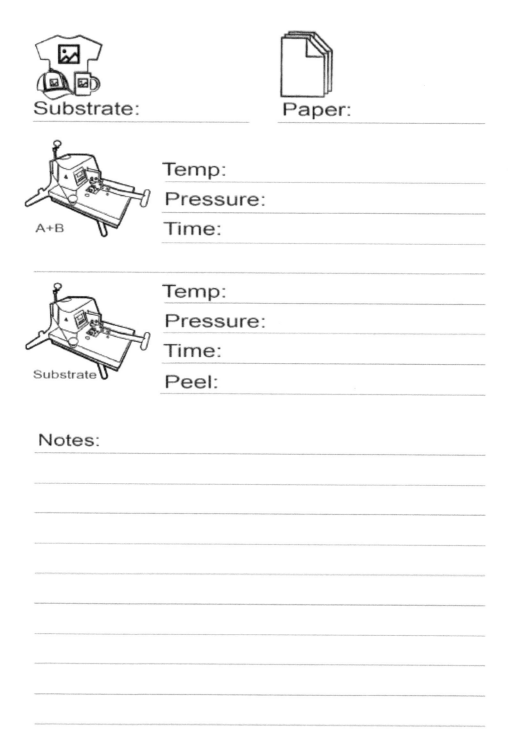

Substrate:

Paper:

A+B

Temp:

Pressure:

Time:

Substrate

Temp:

Pressure:

Time:

Peel:

Notes:

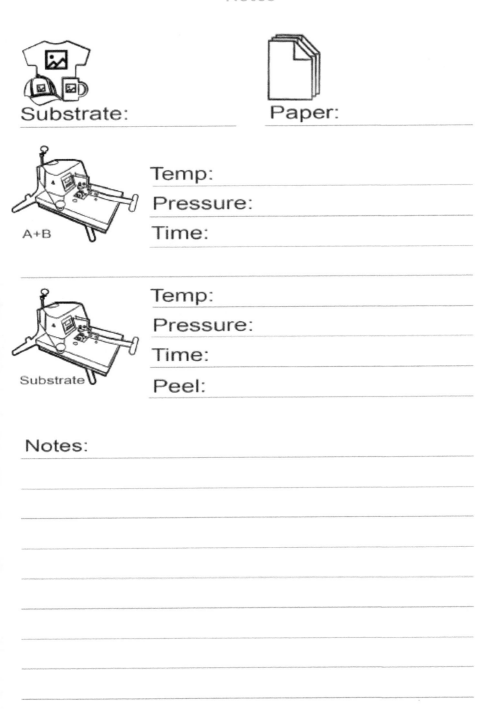

Substrate: _____

Paper: _____

A+B

Temp: _____
Pressure: _____
Time: _____

Substrate

Temp: _____
Pressure: _____
Time: _____
Peel: _____

Notes:
_____
_____
_____
_____
_____
_____
_____
_____
_____

Substrate: _____

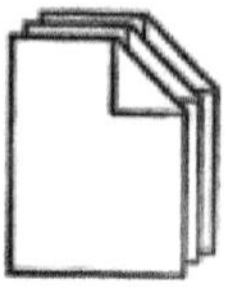

Paper: _____

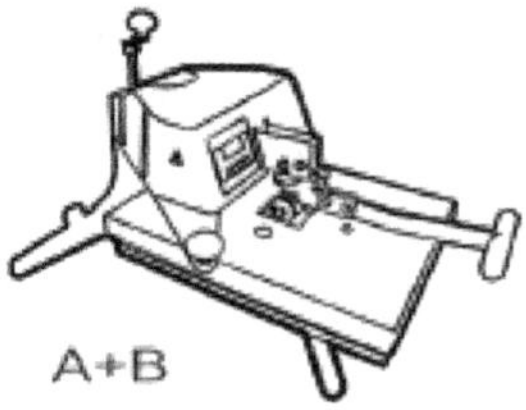

A+B

Temp: _____

Pressure: _____

Time: _____

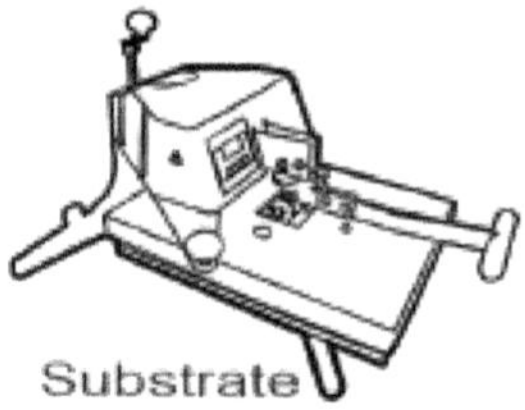

Substrate

Temp: _____

Pressure: _____

Time: _____

Peel: _____

Notes: _____

_____

_____

_____

_____

_____

_____

_____

_____

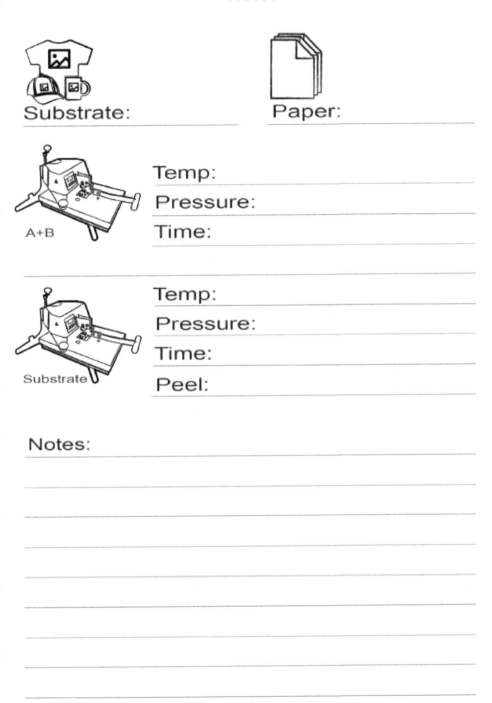

Substrate:

Paper:

Temp:

Pressure:

A+B

Time:

Temp:

Pressure:

Time:

Substrate

Peel:

Notes:

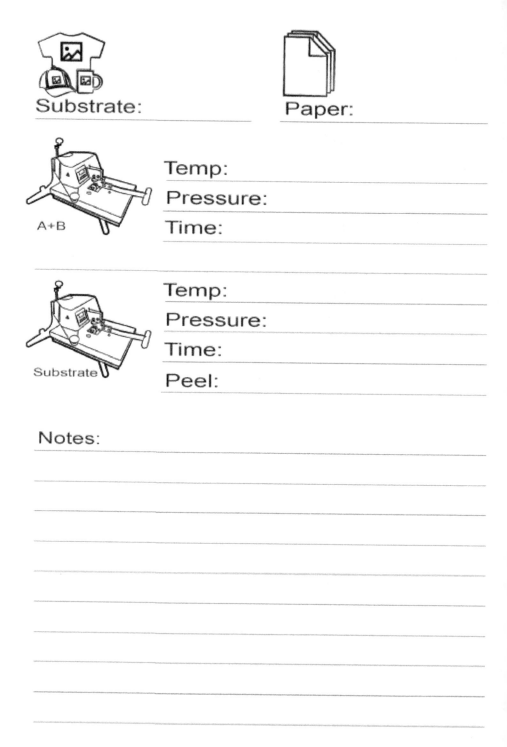

Substrate:

Paper:

Temp:

Pressure:

Time:

A+B

Temp:

Pressure:

Time:

Substrate

Peel:

Notes:

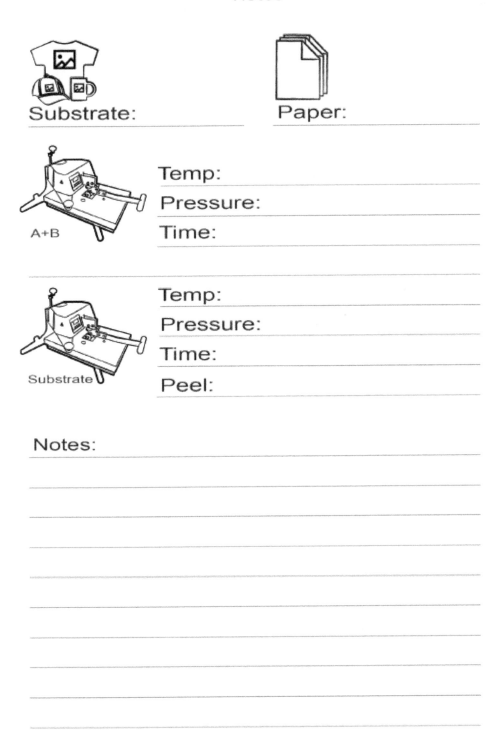

Substrate: _____

Paper: _____

A+B

Temp: _____

Pressure: _____

Time: _____

Substrate

Temp: _____

Pressure: _____

Time: _____

Peel: _____

Notes: _____
_____
_____
_____
_____
_____
_____
_____
_____
_____

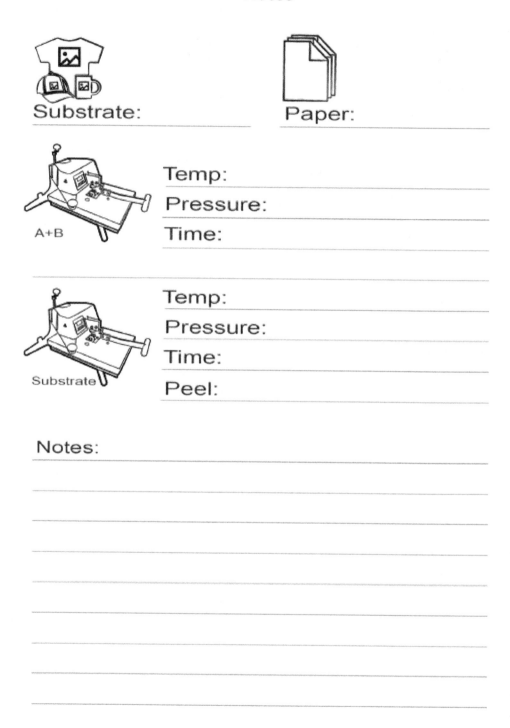

Substrate: _____

Paper: _____

A+B

Temp: _____

Pressure: _____

Time: _____

Substrate

Temp: _____

Pressure: _____

Time: _____

Peel: _____

Notes: _____

_____

_____

_____

_____

_____

_____

_____

_____

_____

Substrate: _____

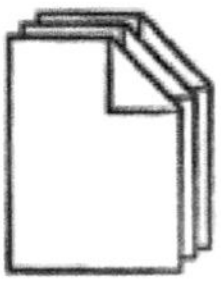

Paper: _____

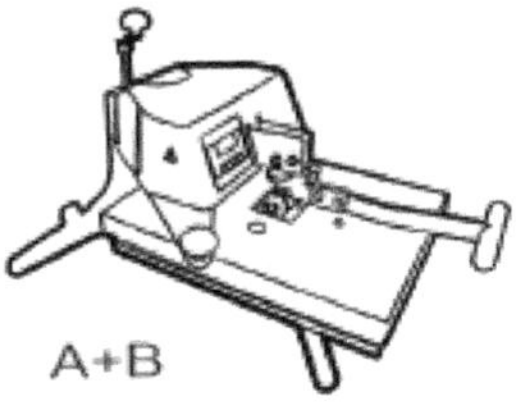

Temp: _____

Pressure: _____

A+B

Time: _____

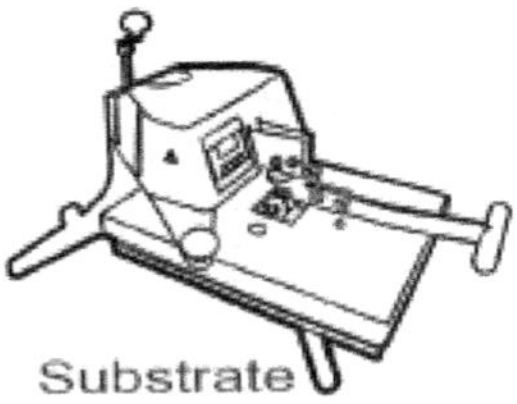

Temp: _____

Pressure: _____

Time: _____

Substrate

Peel: _____

Notes:

_____

_____

_____

_____

_____

_____

_____

_____

_____

_____

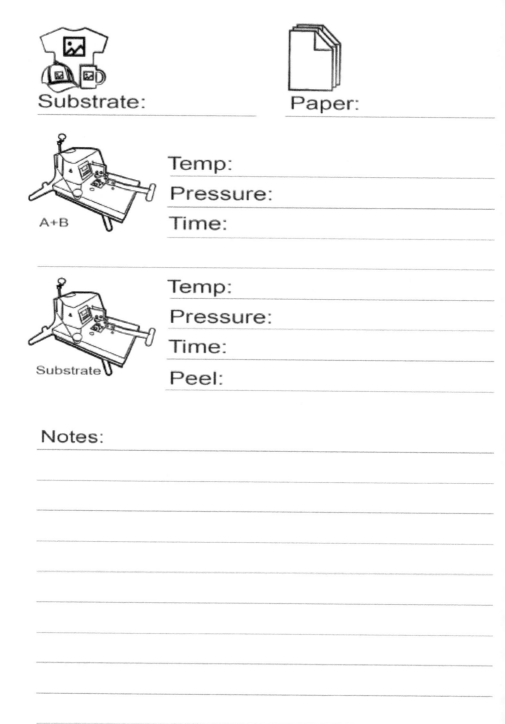

Substrate: _____

Paper: _____

A+B

Temp: _____

Pressure: _____

Time: _____

Substrate

Temp: _____

Pressure: _____

Time: _____

Peel: _____

Notes: _____

_____

_____

_____

_____

_____

_____

_____

_____

_____

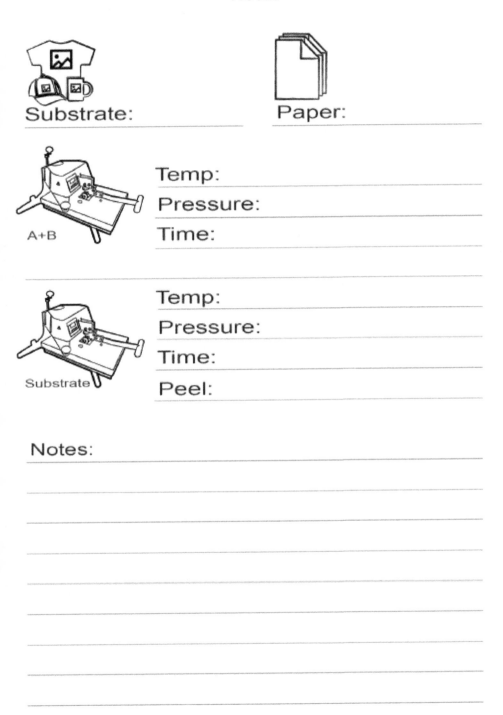

Substrate: _____

Paper: _____

A+B

Temp: _____

Pressure: _____

Time: _____

Substrate

Temp: _____

Pressure: _____

Time: _____

Peel: _____

Notes: _____

_____

_____

_____

_____

_____

_____

_____

_____

_____

_____

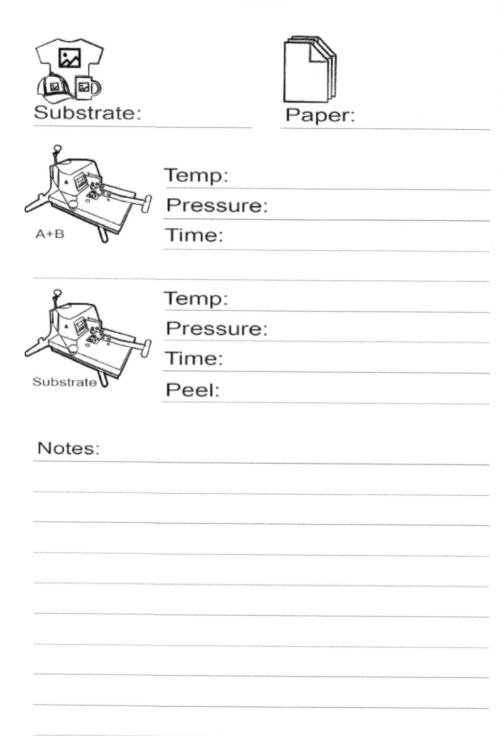

Substrate:

Paper:

A+B

Temp:

Pressure:

Time:

Substrate

Temp:

Pressure:

Time:

Peel:

Notes:

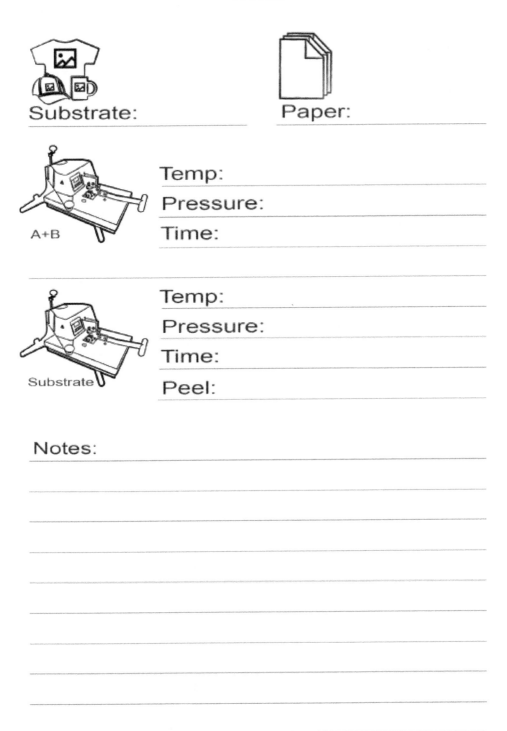

Substrate:

Paper:

Temp:

Pressure:

Time:

A+B

Temp:

Pressure:

Time:

Peel:

Substrate

Notes:

Substrate:

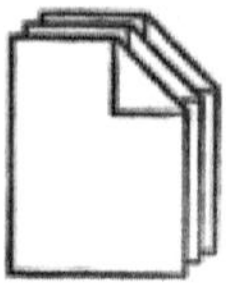

Paper:

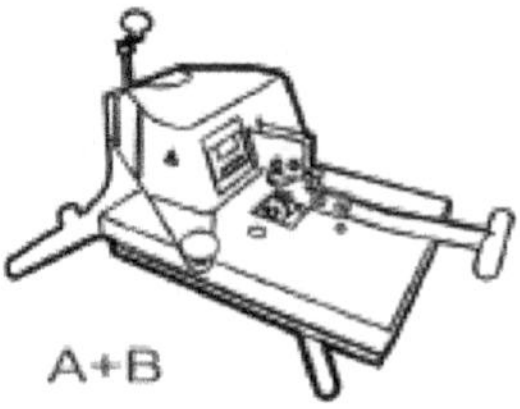

A+B

Temp:

Pressure:

Time:

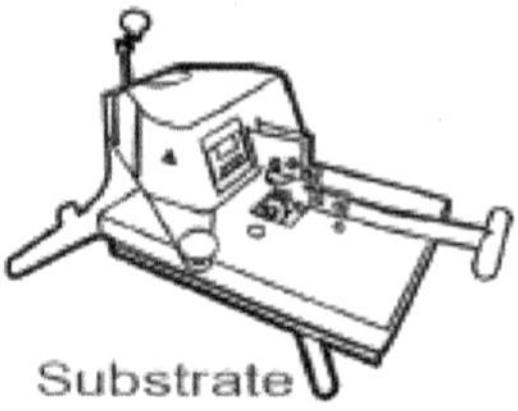

Substrate

Temp:

Pressure:

Time:

Peel:

Notes:

Substrate:

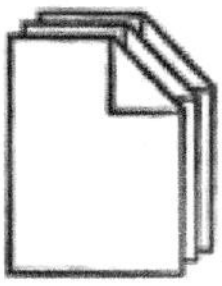

Paper:

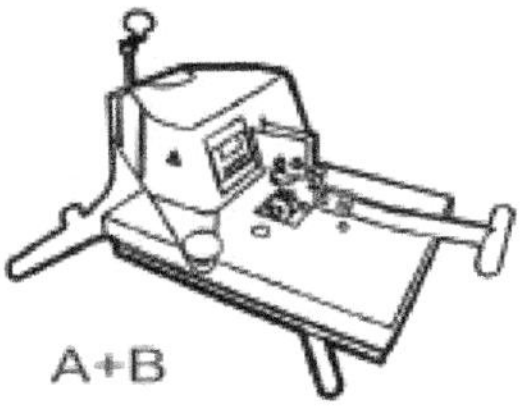

A+B

Temp:

Pressure:

Time:

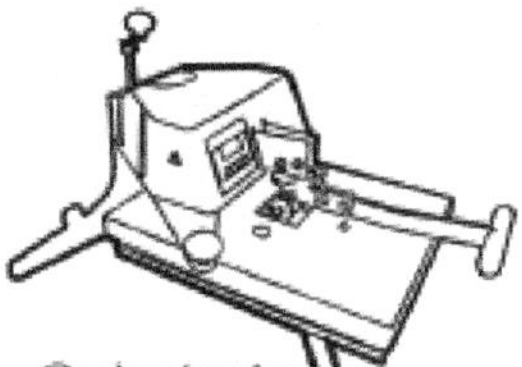

Substrate

Temp:

Pressure:

Time:

Peel:

Notes:

Substrate: 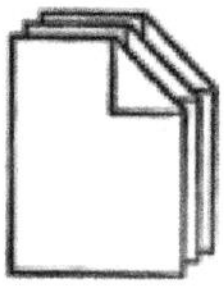 _____   Paper: _____

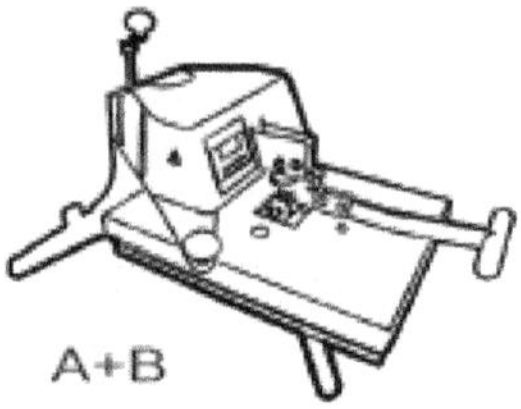

A+B

Temp: _____
Pressure: _____
Time: _____

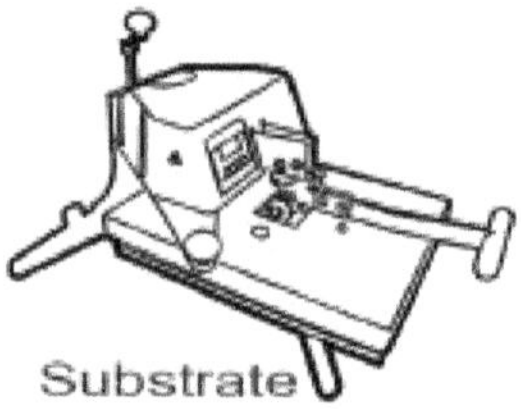

Substrate

Temp: _____
Pressure: _____
Time: _____
Peel: _____

Notes: _____
_____
_____
_____
_____
_____
_____
_____
_____
_____

Substrate: _____

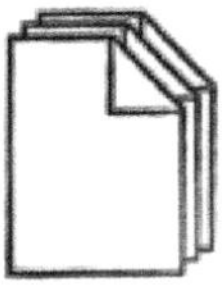

Paper: _____

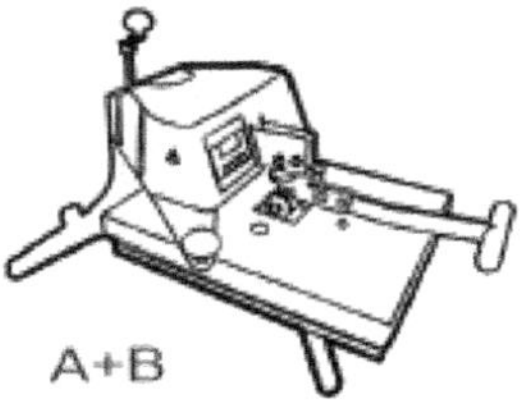

A+B

Temp: _____
Pressure: _____
Time: _____

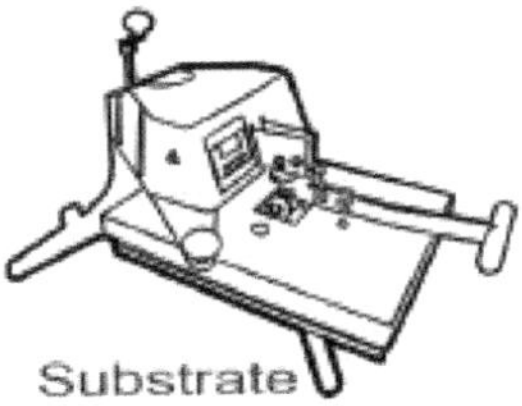

Substrate

Temp: _____
Pressure: _____
Time: _____
Peel: _____

Notes: _____

_____

_____

_____

_____

_____

_____

_____

_____

_____

_____

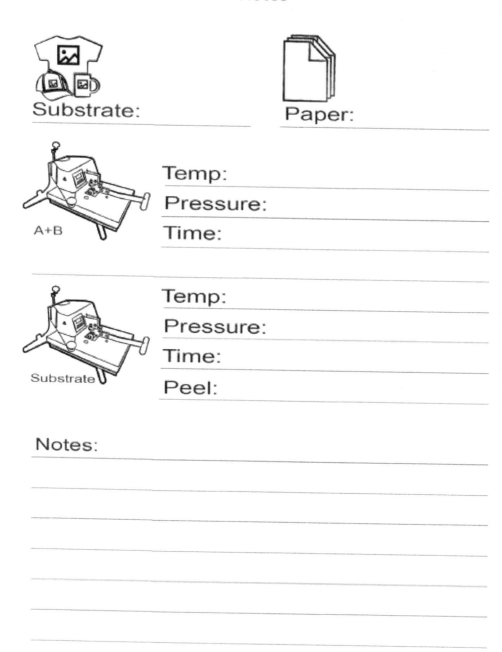

Substrate:

Paper:

A+B

Temp:

Pressure:

Time:

Substrate

Temp:

Pressure:

Time:

Peel:

Notes:

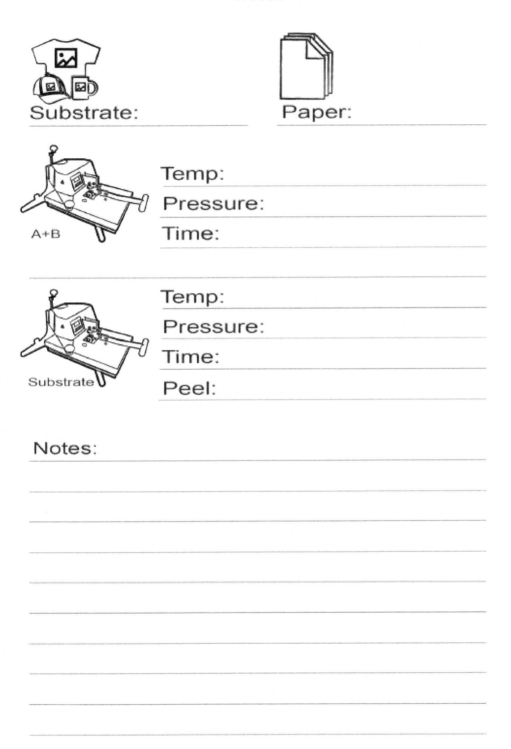

Substrate:

Paper:

Temp:

Pressure:

Time:

A+B

Temp:

Pressure:

Time:

Peel:

Substrate

Notes:

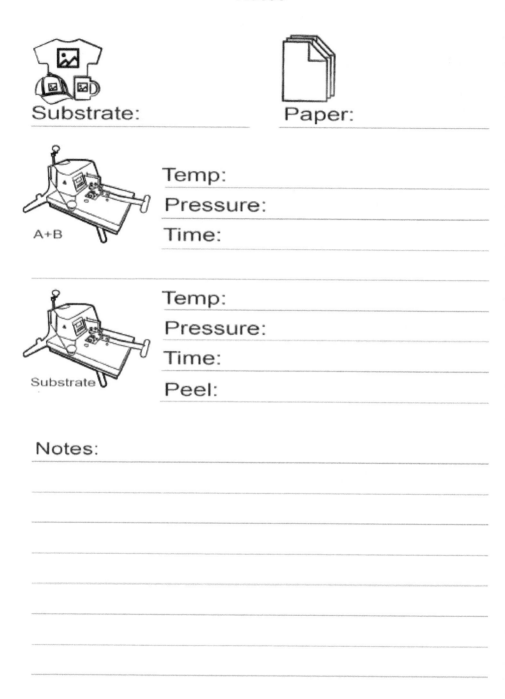

Substrate:

Paper:

A+B

Temp:

Pressure:

Time:

Substrate

Temp:

Pressure:

Time:

Peel:

Notes:

Substrate: 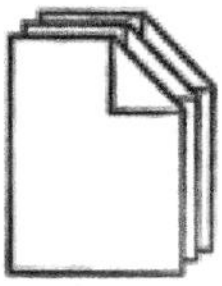 _____   Paper: _____

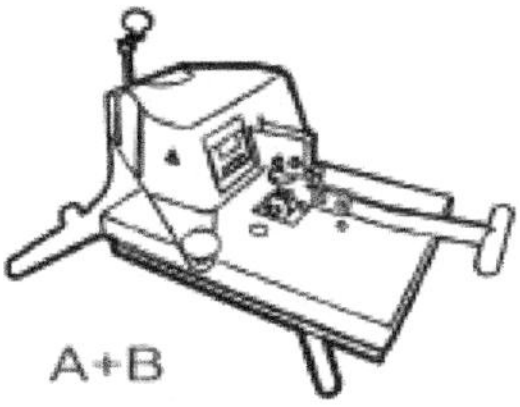

A+B

Temp: _____

Pressure: _____

Time: _____

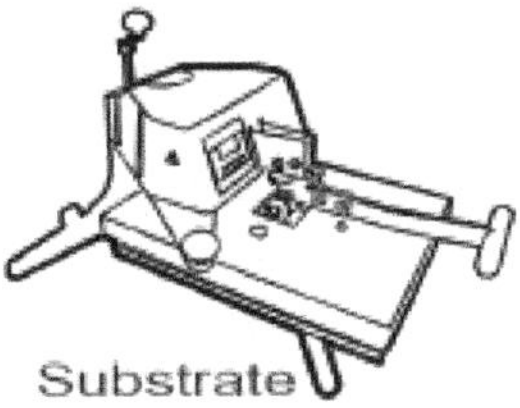

Substrate

Temp: _____

Pressure: _____

Time: _____

Peel: _____

Notes:

_____

_____

_____

_____

_____

_____

_____

_____

_____

_____

Substrate: _____

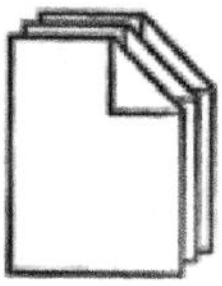

Paper: _____

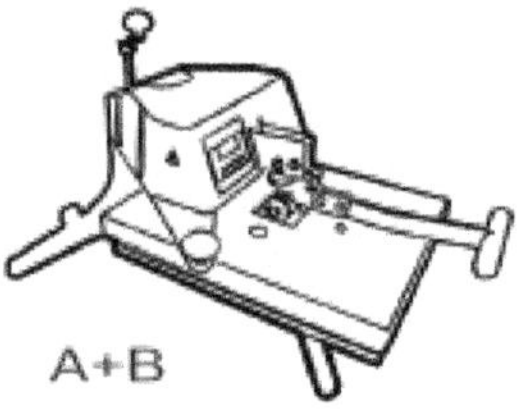

A+B

Temp: _____

Pressure: _____

Time: _____

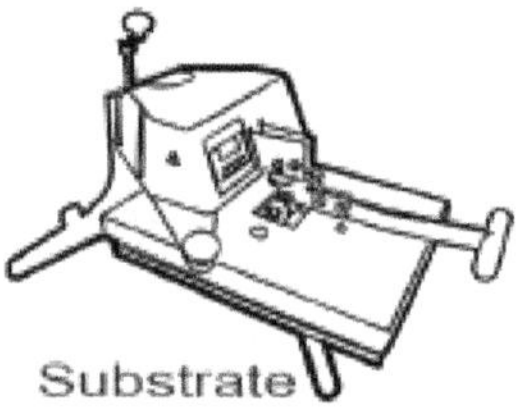

Substrate

Temp: _____

Pressure: _____

Time: _____

Peel: _____

Notes: _____

_____

_____

_____

_____

_____

_____

_____

_____

_____

Substrate:

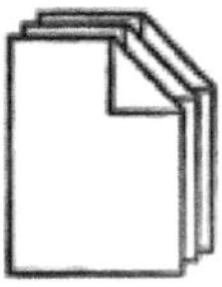

Paper:

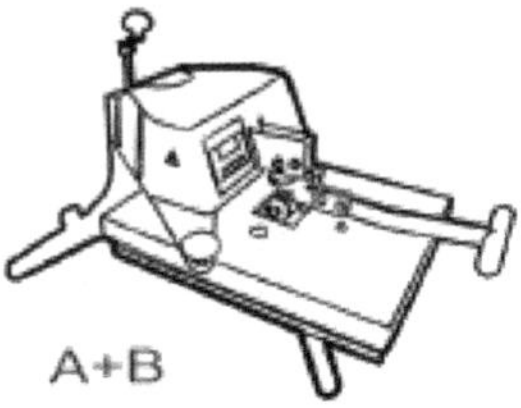

A+B

Temp:

Pressure:

Time:

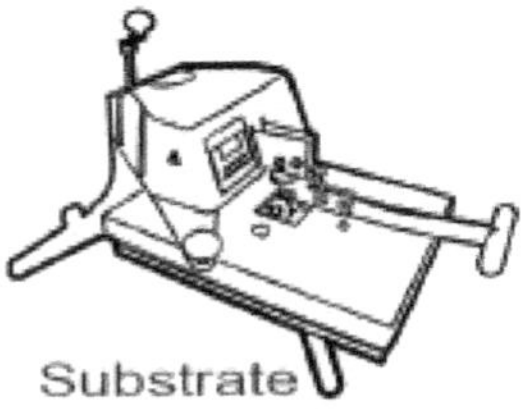

Substrate

Temp:

Pressure:

Time:

Peel:

Notes:

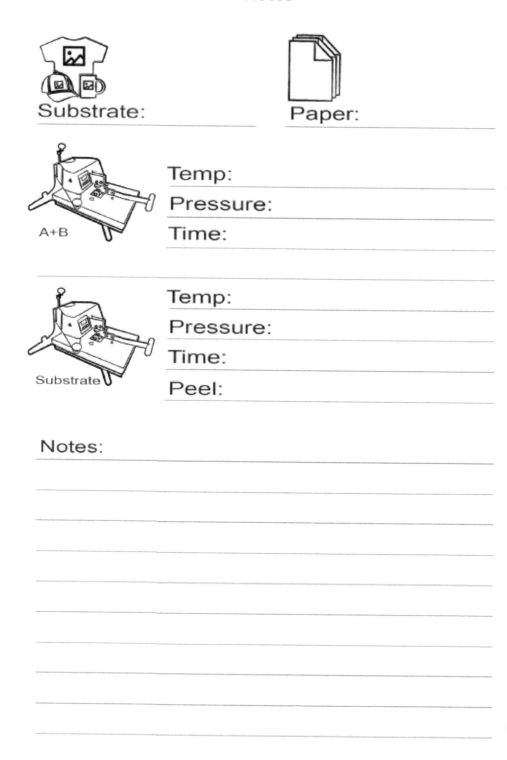

Substrate:

Paper:

A+B

Temp:

Pressure:

Time:

Substrate

Temp:

Pressure:

Time:

Peel:

Notes:

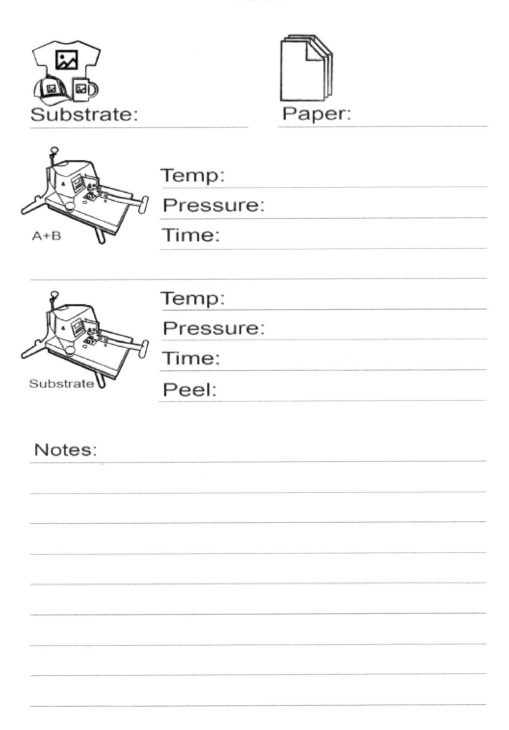

Substrate:

Paper:

A+B

Temp:

Pressure:

Time:

Substrate

Temp:

Pressure:

Time:

Peel:

Notes:

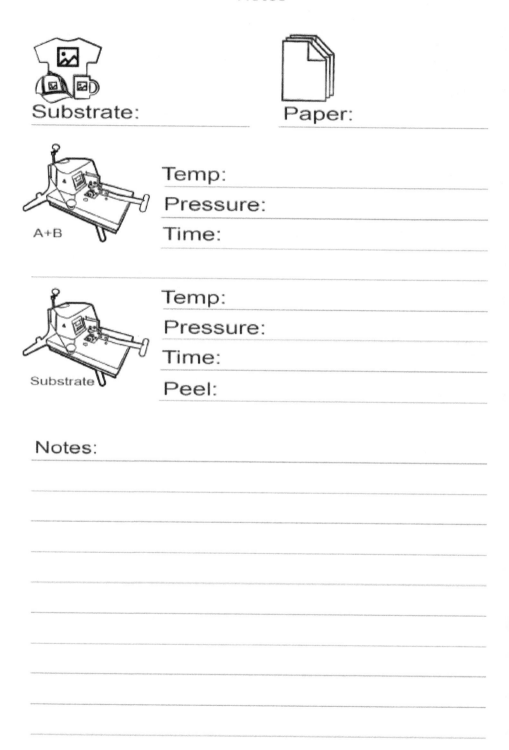

Substrate:

Paper:

Temp:

Pressure:

Time:

A+B

Temp:

Pressure:

Time:

Peel:

Substrate

Notes:

Substrate: _____

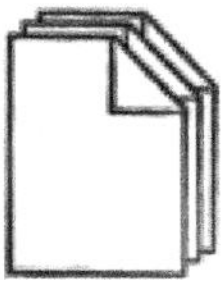

Paper: _____

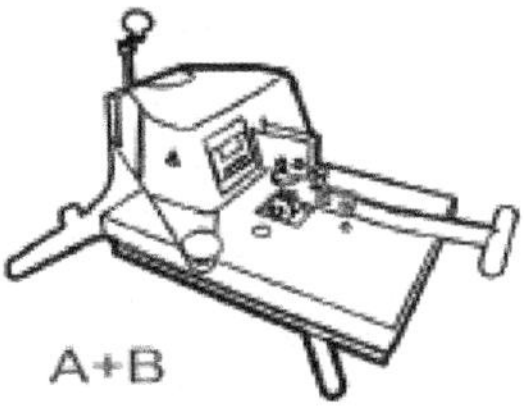

A+B

Temp: _____
Pressure: _____
Time: _____

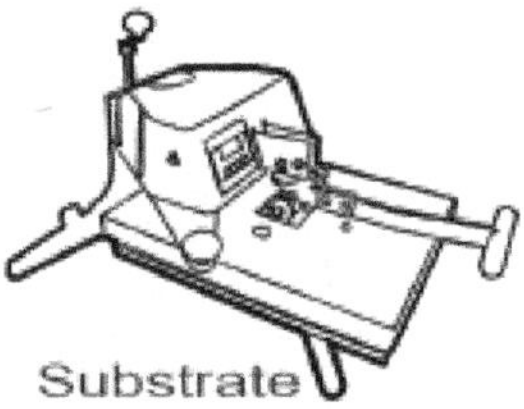

Substrate

Temp: _____
Pressure: _____
Time: _____
Peel: _____

Notes: _____

_____

_____

_____

_____

_____

_____

_____

_____

_____

Substrate:

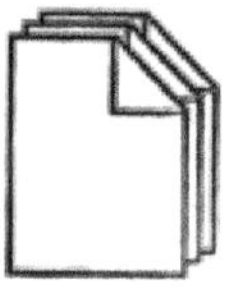

Paper:

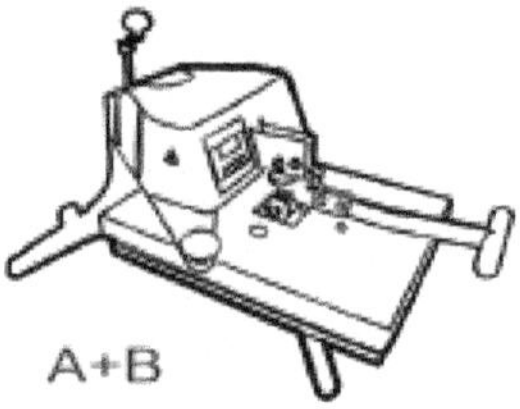

A+B

Temp:
Pressure:
Time:

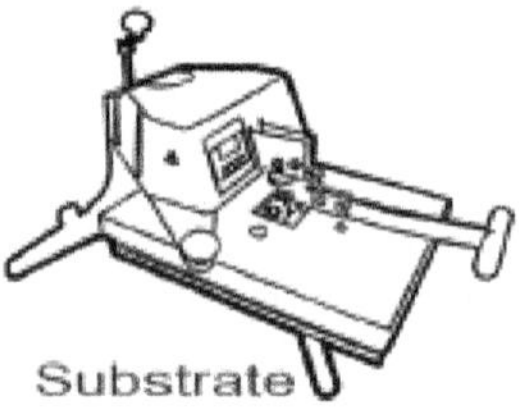

Substrate

Temp:
Pressure:
Time:
Peel:

Notes:

Substrate: 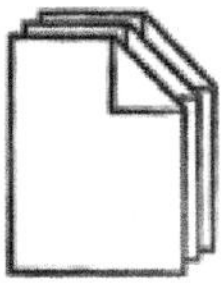 _____   Paper: _____

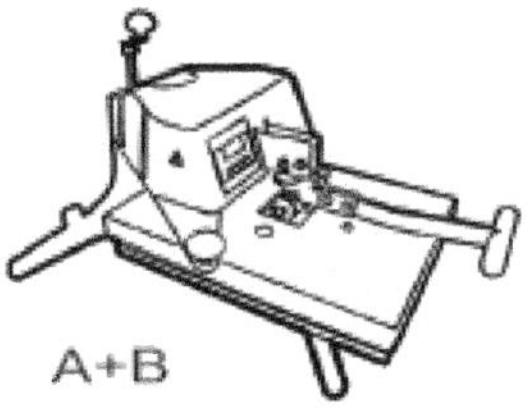

A+B

Temp: _____
Pressure: _____
Time: _____

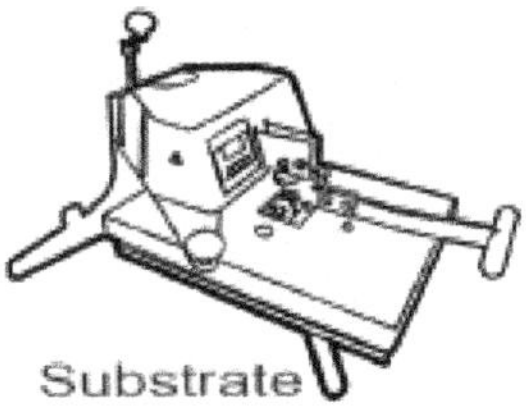

Substrate

Temp: _____
Pressure: _____
Time: _____
Peel: _____

Notes: _____

_____

_____

_____

_____

_____

_____

_____

_____

_____

_____

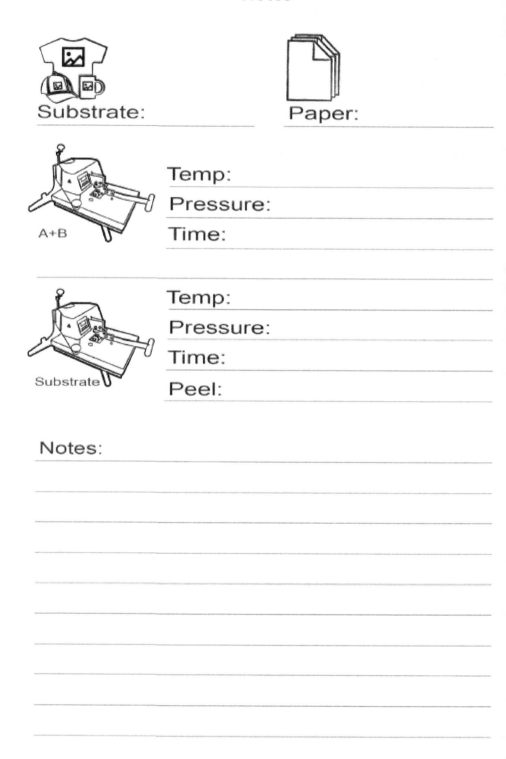

Substrate:

Paper:

A+B

Temp:

Pressure:

Time:

Substrate

Temp:

Pressure:

Time:

Peel:

Notes:

This Notebook belongs to:

Name: _____

Address: _____

Phone: _____

www.icolorprint.com

Made in the USA
Monee, IL
01 October 2021